HOMELESSNESS AND ADDICTION
IN LONDON IN THE 1960S

By

Nigel Miller

Kevern, a former school friend, was studying to be a priest. He became acquainted with the brothers of the Church of England who worked at the church of Saint Botolph without Aldgate in the east end of London. The rector was the Reverend Derek Harbord, formerly Mister Justice Harbord. Beneath the church was a crypt which was divided into two parts. One part was a centre for the homeless; the other part was used as a youth club in the evenings and later as a lunch club for city workers. The two parts were linked by a door but were kept separate and those who attended one part did not enter the other.

During the holidays Kevern asked me if I would be interested in visiting the centres. On 25 June 1964 I went there with him. I had a cup of tea with Brother Richard, Brother Garry, Peter who was the verger and George who was the gardener. I attended Matins and then helped to serve tea and soup to the down and outs. After lunch in the Toc H canteen I helped to pair some shoes. As Garry had to go to feed his Alsatian dog I looked after the kitchen until he came back. I went back to the store where Kevern was fitting out some people with clothes and helped to arrange some garments.

At lunch the Brothers said that when they first worked at the centre and the down and outs arrived to be served they asked themselves, "What next?" I said I had that feeling. The face of one man was covered in grime like that of a coal man. Kevern said that those who hadn't been on the streets long still washed but after a while they no longer did so. Another man's eye appeared to have been cut out deliberately for the raw flesh was visible.

The down and outs who came were single people. Occasionally I saw a couple on the streets who seemed down and out and assumed they were husband and wife. Over the course of time I found that most of the homeless appreciated what was done for them and as they left they thanked the helper but there a few exceptions. Some were alcoholics or meths drinkers. One man came in drunk and wanted new clothes and a shave. He was asked to come back sober to get what he wanted. I referred to him as "the drunk" when I tried to identify him but Brother Richard reminded me that we all had our problems. Asking him to come back sober for new clothes gave him an incentive not to get drunk again.

A man in crutches came and demanded a new suit but was told to wash the one he had which made him furious. I said that we didn't collect all that much money and he said he didn't care how much money we collected. He threw his crutches at Brother Garry and had to be told to go out. Occasionally a man shouted obscenities at a helper and was asked to leave. A female helper was upset when she was on the receiving end. Brother John (who also worked in the centre but whom I met later) said he wasn't concerned by down and outs using foul language as they didn't know any better but was annoyed if other people did so.

Sometimes a homeless person offered to help. When the centre was closing and the floor was to be swept one man said he would do that. Brother John said he would see about getting him a job. I don't remember seeing the man again and wonder if he did get a job and settle down.

The brothers said that over the course of time they formed a relationship with the men which meant they could help them with problems. During the winter the police asked them for help in identifying people found dead on the streets. As a casual helper I only got to know a few.

The brothers did say they didn't give anyone money as it might be spent on drink or drugs. A man asked them to give him money for a bus fare. Brother John offered to buy him a ticket on the bus but the man wanted the money. John asked him what difference it made if he bought the ticket instead of giving him the money and the man replied that he wanted to ask for the ticket himself. I suggested that he would spend the money on something stronger. He assured me it he wouldn't but we all knew he would. The man continued to refuse the offer and when the crypt closed at the end of the afternoon he was left seated alone at the entrance.

Similar problems occurred when children claimed they had lost their bus fare and asked for money. Before I worked at the centre a boy asked me for his bus fare but told me inflated amount and ran off when I queried it. Since then I learned to offer to buy a ticket and if they were genuine they would gratefully accept.

I also helped out at the Youth Club. Harry King, who had started the down and out centre, was the youth leader and Brother Garry assisted him. Garry told me the rough type came; about one third of the members had been to prison and another third regularly went inside; some smoked reefers in the toilets and others did it openly. The female members were "semi prostitutes" and some had babies; others were responsible for trouble. The purpose of the club was to stop the kids becoming down and outs.

The first time I served apprehensively behind the bar. A fair haired girl had an unpleasant manner and Garry told her not to be rude. Someone else asked me if he could pay for the drinks the following night. I said, "No." and he accepted that. I had been told to serve drinks only in a glass. The reason was that some members had used broken bottles to attack others. Someone helped himself from a bottle and I asked him to put it in a glass. He told me he was a helper and added, "I don't want anything from you, mate." Garry was called and he told me he would give me a hand if necessary. His companion, who seemed friendly, came over to ask me what the problem was and I told him. He said, "Johnny's a queer boy." I might have handled the situation better if I had called Garry over first. Two members complained that some chocolate was mouldy and Garry assured them it was perfectly all right. Tuesday was normally a quiet night and despite the problem I coped.

Sometime later Harry King said he knew "Johnny" had blown up. He knew how difficult it was for Harry to get helpers and wanted to apologise. He wasn't really a bad sort but was easily led.

Another night a West Indian who had no money wanted to owe. I called Garry over. The West Indian may have wanted to walk off with his drinks. Another helped, Bill, joined in and one of the glasses was spilt. The West Indian used an expletive and said he had put on a clean shirt that night which was now stained by juice. He said something about "this man" to Garry who said he would have to pay for the spilled drink. He agreed reluctantly and shook hands about it but he was far from happy. Harry said that "Bullets" was not too bad a character but he never forgot about the spilled drink. Looking back I think the scrap at the bar could have been avoided.

After heavy rain the crypt was flooded. Garry considered calling the fire brigade but they would have been answering lots of calls. Members arrived and

"David", a helper who collected the money at the door,
opened it and said the club wasn't open. The fair haired
girl snapped, "You might have told us last night." The
curate went out and explained that the crypt was flooded.
He came back and said she just turned up her nose. Garry
said, "This is the type we're dealing with."

Later Harry came and pulled up a drain which allowed
the water to flow away. If he had been there earlier the
flood would have been avoided. Because of the flood the
club didn't open for another half an hour and Garry and I
went for a late supper. When I returned Bill was serving
behind the bar and I was left with nothing to do. The kids
weren't the sociable type and I wasn't able to make contact
with anyone. Several months later someone came and
asked if the club was for members only and I said it
wasn't. He paid to come in and later I noticed him sitting
alone. The members weren't the kind who went out of
their way to make new arrivals feel welcome. He may
have only just moved to London and knew nobody. I
should have warned him about the club.

The police came in with a photo of Margaret
Harrington, a missing girl, and asked if anyone knew her
whereabouts. I asked a police woman where the photo was
taken or wasn't I supposed to know that. She said it was
taken in Hyde Park. I said I didn't know her; she asked me
if I was sure and I said I was. After showing the photo to
everyone the police shone a torch in the homeless centre

which was in darkness. I didn't think she would hide in there. Garry said occasionally the police did come in about missing people.

I helped "David" take the money at the door. He told me he could have Garry thrown out of the brotherhood (he could have just been saying that) but wouldn't do anything like that to Harry as Harry had been very good to him. At a later date "David" told others that he had been a tramp and because of Harry he had rebuilt his life. They did have their rows but basically got on. He also told me he had contacts with all walks of life and could find out everything about anyone. He could easily find out where I lived within a few days; I might not think anyone was following me but someone might be. When he was away others took over the place where he lived and he had nowhere to go, so he took appropriate action.

The club had been closed for four weeks and it was quiet. Brother Garry had gone to Yorkshire for training. Harry said he had barred "David" although he admitted he had made a good job of taking the money at the door.

One night I stepped outside and had an opportunity to speak to two girls and a boy. I was glad about that and Harry seemed pleased.

Another night I wanted someone to put his drink in a glass but he was furious and called me a stupid idiot (no four letter words). Harry said it was all right to him to drink from the bottle. He said that all he wanted to do was to come in and smoke weed and didn't want any trouble. Later he offered to shake hands and we did so. Harry was concerned that we were all right. Afterwards he was friendly whenever he met me although he was said to have a reputation as a terror. Kevern said what had happened meant I had got to know him.

I went to the club and found it had been closed for five nights because older people had been admitted (the age limit was supposed to be 21) and too many drugged cigarettes had been smoked.

On the first night in January that the club was open new membership cards were issued. Maximum age limit of 19 and minimum age limit of 14 were to be enforced but in practice older people still entered.

A member "Billy" said that the reason for the rise in the crime rate was that the police have to arrest a certain number of people each month and to do so they have to frame people. A police officer had recently been charged with framing suspects and I asked "Billy" for an example wondering if he would mention that officer but "Billy" replied, "Me".

Brother Garry was replaced by Brother Lawrence. When he was trying to do his job some members attacked him and broke his glasses. Harry warned the members that the rector would take a dim view of a brother being attacked and might close the club. However it wasn't closed; Lawrence acclimatised himself and became friendly with one of the attackers. After he had left Harry met that boy in the street and he asked how Lawrence was.

A girl whom I hadn't seen before was at the club. Harry said she might seem a nice girl but she had beaten some girls up and they hadn't been coming. Another time she showed me a sore place on her arm. I didn't ask her how she got it but it may have been during a fight. She asked if she could pay for a drink at a later date. I told her to ask Brother Lawrence if that was all right. She went over to him and he clearly said, "No" but she returned and told me he said, "Yes". When I didn't give her the drink she displayed her personality. When some fruit juice was splashed on her by mistake she pulled the lead out of the kettle and held it against me as if to electrocute me. Lawrence told her that was not in the least bit funny.

Mr King also operated the lunch club with Trudi Eulenburg. One city worker complained that the cheese was rotten (c. f. The complaint about the mouldy chocolate). A few members of the youth club came to the lunch club although their presence was discouraged. Some older people were uncomplimentary about the conduct of the younger people but was there ever a time when the older generation didn't complain about the younger?

Somebody came to the lunch club and enquired about

the work that the people in the crypt were doing. Mr King related an incident when he visited a family about their son. On the table were some pep pills and he was asked, "Harry, like a pill?" He realised he was wasting his time with them. After she had left he said he hadn't meant to tell her so much; she was probably someone who was writing a book.

Harry King had worked in the building trade at one time and as he planned to return there they advertised for another youth leader. From several applicants George Iggleton was chosen. He said he didn't think "the east end (of London) kids" were any worse than any others and Harry said he would do a lot of good with them. He allocated them a number and when they came again asked them what it was; some owned up to the same number. He organised a table tennis tournament. Some who played in the first round didn't come again; others who were substituted didn't come either and in the end the tournament was abandoned.

Mr Iggleton encountered difficulties. He put two girls out for not paying. It was unfair for some people to pay while others would get away without but after that the girls kept away. A down and out entered the club and the members ragged him and played the fool. Harry wouldn't have let him in. The club suffered from an excess of helpers. They played cards so that they wouldn't sit around doing nothing. Harry admitted that one helper did more harm than good although the members told her their backgrounds; she passed the information on to him which was of some value. A crowd came from Toynbee Hall; they got in the way and encouraged immature behaviour whereas all would have gone smoothly. George stood there preferring to do nothing but Harry would have taken action. Harry agreed that the crowd did more harm than good. It was an excellent example of too many cooks spoiling the broth.

Harry said that two members who had been in prison for 18 months entered the club. When George asked them to pay they told him where to get off. If he had persisted they would have assaulted him (as had happened to Brother Lawrence). They must have been involved in violence as on a previous occasion one of them said that his friend had been involved in more punch ups than he had.

Fewer people were attending which seemed to be a general trend with clubs at that time. A hard core came regularly, some came for a while and others came only once or twice possibly because they didn't like it, or became bored with it or ended up in prison. One night when the club was closing early because of lack of numbers a police officer came in. He was told the club was about to close and seemed disappointed. Harry had said the club had been raided for drugs and I wondered if the police had been planning a raid. Two youths who were smoking reefers turned round to hide them. The officer left without realising that and may have been too concerned about the ruined plans to be observant.

Mr King returned to the building trade. Later Miss Eulenburg told me that Mr Iggleton had been asked to take over the running of the club. She thought he could have taken over but he decided not to. He may have been used to a suburban youth club and would have carried out valuable work. He would have had a good influence on teenagers who were troublesome but had little experience of facing those who were violent, smoked reefers or were drug addicts. His approach would have worked in the suburbs but not in the east end of London. If he had been able to run the club under Harry's guidance for a while all might have been different.

Both the youth club and the centre for the homeless were closed in the latter case because the brothers moved on. Later the centre reopened a few evenings a week but the club didn't yet reopen although the Bishop of London wanted it too. However I believe the club remained closed and in later years the centre occupied the whole of the crypt.

I understood the police had wanted the place to be shut permanently because of the drug taking. What was surprising was that a P C Jolley, a dog handler, used to come in with his Alsatian dog and talk to some of the younger members. It was an excellent dog and came first in some kind of police competition. The runner up came from Southend on Sea which was a good force. He didn't seem concerned about the kids smoking reefers openly. I wondered if his superiors had any idea what he was doing and, if they did, whether they approved. He might have been carrying out surveillance without anyone realising it and passing on the information.

Whether it was a good thing for the club to close was a matter of opinion. Harry King did command respect among the members. One of the two violent men wouldn't move out of the way when a helper asked him but said he would do so if Harry asked him. The members usually behaved themselves in the club premises although there were exceptions as when Brother Lawrence was assaulted and broken bottles had been known to be used to attack others. When some youths planned a wages snatch Harry talked them out of it. What might otherwise have happened was a matter of speculation. He had trusted another member and allowed him to be behind the bar but that member kicked an old lady to death. When he had to go into hospital the club was thought to have to close but the members came to see him and promised to cooperate during his absence; it therefore remained open. The only problem was that towards the end the record player was stolen.

Harry said most of the kids didn't have any respect for authority nor for anyone who was prepared to work and get on in life. From about 12 years of age they went around in gangs. Kids in gangs could be found in the suburbs or even in rural areas and they might intimidate people but they didn't compare with the urban gangs. If it was a choice between the gangs being on the streets or in the club the latter would be preferable. Those who can influence them are a rare breed and after Harry left the rector told me that few people had his flair.

Because of the type who came in Harry had to warn helpers to be on their guard for things being stolen. One lady had her handbag pinched which meant that members were not allowed to go behind the bar except for the few who could be trusted. However other tactics could be employed. Someone might approach the bar and say he wanted a glass of water (reefer smoking did make people thirsty). While someone else was getting the water another person would take some items that were for sale. Another trick was to remove an item and pass it on. Harry said they may think they were clever but they were idiots.

The quickness of the hand deceived the eye. If the helper was taking some money and giving change Harry warned him not to leave the money on the counter.

Removing money or anything else when someone was watching might appear difficult but they were trained in that. He said that he visited "Bullets" in prison and a packet of cigarettes on the table. He took them without Harry or the warder noticing.

Not all who came in were undesirable people. Harry said that a bus driver was a very nice chap and I found a metal welder was friendly.

Some were not what they might seem. One member carried out some valuable work in the down and out centre. Sometimes he gave me a lift to the station and appeared to be a decent person. He disappeared and Harry said he had left the area because he was in trouble. I said I thought he was all right and Harry said that was "his passport to fame". Someone else "Stewart" told some helpers he worked for a cleaner but he wasn't the type whom anyone would employ. He had annoyed another helper and Harry had previously told me to watch him. One girl "Pamela" told me she had obtained four O levels and worked in the Stock Exchange. Harry doubted the truth of what she said although she did seem to be a better type of girl; she didn't give the impression she was lying and you could carry on a sensible conversation with her. Nevertheless you did have to be wary of what you were told. Someone said that he had been serving behind the bar when I was still at school but he wasn't the sort who would be asked to do that. Later in life I found you also had to be wary about what some professional people told you.

A member who brought records to the club said he had let me take a record on the understanding I would pay for it another time. I said that wasn't me and he appeared to accept that. Afterwards he insisted that was me and became threatening. In the end he didn't pursue the matter and trusted me to keep an item behind the bar for him. Later I mentioned to Harry that he had lost one of his records and Harry said he was trying to get me to pay for something he knew I hadn't taken and I should have mentioned that.

I had asked Harry what the best way of getting on with the members was and he said it was let them do their own thing. As already observed the kids generally didn't try to be sociable and it was difficult to know how to communicate unless a specific opportunity arose (although the same might be said for other places). My experience with the two girls and a boy was an exception. I was also able to have a conversation with the bus driver and the metal welder. George said you could try talking about a specific event. In the Readers Digest was an article about a disastrous football match that ended up in violence and he suggested I could bring that into a conversation. However you couldn't walk up to someone and start talking about it or any other topic without a reason.

If you did have an opportunity to hold a conversation what the kids said could be rubbish and repetitive. One member came to the door and said, "I'm skint." in a childish manner meaning he had no money to pay to come in. One helper complained that they didn't talk sense. One youth called himself "Bootsy" because he didn't anyone to know his real name. If they ordered food or drink then it was almost prepared they were liable to say "Cancel it" although they still wanted it. Brother Lawrence commented that if the mental ages of the older members were the same as their actual ages they wouldn't want to come into a place like this.

How do people end up homeless, drunkards or drug addicts? Much has already been written. Those who ran the centre for the down and outs said they may have relied on someone else and when that person was no longer there they couldn't cope and ended up on the streets. Others couldn't stand the pressures of their job or modern life and started drinking.

It was known for youngsters to take drugs because of the kind of homes they came from. One boy smoked reefers, took pep pills and was in danger of ending up on the hard drugs. His brother originally wasn't seen with a reefer but later smoked them. Mr King spoke to their father who said he was on the pills. In fact the father was worse than his boys but the mother was a good woman.

Children were in danger of becoming drug addicts or drunkards by copying their parents.

During the First World War soldiers were shattered by their experiences even if they hadn't been injured or taken prisoner. They vented their feelings onto their children who passed them onto the grandchildren. They might not always be violent but constantly moaning at or criticising children made them indirectly war casualties and harmed them mentally. They justified the children's unhappiness by saying, "I had to go through the war." The children couldn't make a success of their job or may have ended up in a job where they were miserable. They had become incapable neither of forming relationships nor of generating respect and had nobody to confide in. Eventually they decided they would be better off living on the streets. The result could occur when people were caught up in other conflicts or similar experiences in other spheres of life.

Some down and outs had been doctors or lawyers; the voice of one man indicated he may have been a colonel or a major. They found the pressures of their job too much or had taken on more work than they could manage. After drinking two glasses of wine at a party their anxieties became matters that weren't important and would sort themselves out. For that reason they drank two glasses at other times but soon two glasses no longer created the desired effect and they had to drink more. When wine no longer satisfied they moved onto stronger drinks such as gin and could even end up drinking meths. Alcohol may have steadied them at first but without out it what were anxieties had become enormous worries and they were forced to drink more to be in the position when they started. Others may have smoked a couple of reefers to steady themselves which also sent them on a downward spiral.

The indirect war casualties might have started drinking or taking drugs as a means of escape from their awful home life and job. They dare not admit to their families that they couldn't cope and were becoming alcoholics or addicts. In other cases people drank a few glasses at ordinary social gatherings which might seem harmless but later found they couldn't control their drinking. They might attempt to hide their addiction. If anyone noticed a change in them they would say they had a cold or a headache or they had a troublesome matter to deal with and soon everything would be all right. It was only a question of time before their work was affected and disaster struck at the office; they lost their job and home and had to live on the streets.

It was possible to be in business with someone else that milked it or carried out dishonest financial transactions. By the time the other realised what had happened it was too late. The business crashed and the innocent party also lost his livelihood and his home. If he had no family or friends to support him he might end up on the streets through no fault of his own.

After I went to my first sherry party and had two glasses problems no longer mattered. The next time two glasses didn't have the same effect. Fortunately I didn't regularly attend parties and was able to avoid alcohol. However the line between ending up and not ending up homeless is fine. Many people, including me, realise how close they came to homelessness, drug addiction, or alcoholism and it was only through luck they didn't.

In the mid-1960s a Labour government was in power. The people who ran the centre were Labour party supporters and didn't blame government policies. Of course I have no means of knowing who they would have blamed if there had been a Conservative government. Blaming governments did become fashionable in later years when the Conservatives were in power. Somebody said that despair through government policies was the cause.

Young people were introduced to cigarettes. When I was a teenager I was told that smoking was a nice social activity. At school a master said that if someone was offered a cigarette and then said, "No thank you; I don't smoke." there was a slight cold wind. However he didn't suggest smoking was a good thing and that the pupils ought to start. Later when I said I didn't smoke I was told that I might end up smoking through social pressures. Youngsters smoked because their friends smoked. Reefers were passed round at teenage parties and when they were offered a reefer they might smoke it. If they refused they would be called "chicken". One helper at the youth club had a steady job but decided to smoke reefers to find out what it was like. For some reason she telephoned an organisation to say she had started that in the club. After that she was barred. Of course not all people who smoke cigarettes start to smoke reefers but what the helper did does show the danger.

Some people start because of their social environment. Harry King told me that in the West Indies 65% of the population smoked reefers because it wasn't a crime in that country although the government intended to take action. He had known all the family including the children to smoke them. One West Indian told a helper that his mother gave him one when he was twelve. I asked Harry whether those who had jobs, such as on the buses and trains, smoked reefers and he said most of them didn't although they might when they were off duty. One club member said he obtained them from the West Indians. Of course many people who smoke them aren't from the West Indies.

A few down and outs were Scottish. I didn't know how they ended up on the streets of London but wonder whether they enjoyed a fair life in their home town but travelled to London hoping for a better life. Nothing worked out, they couldn't return home, may have taken to drink or drugs and became homeless. One of the two club members who had been involved in punch ups spoke with what seemed to be a welsh accent. He may have travelled to London for the same reason but became involved with a bad lot. He hadn't had any contact with his parents for some time but didn't say why. Other young people had travelled to London because they were bored with home life and wished for something better but found everything far worse and finished up on drink or drugs. Later did that club member ever think about his home and miss his family, former friends and familiar places now no longer there for him?

Parents had been known to move to another area, because of change of job, retirement or other reasons, and leave a teenager behind to fend for himself or herself. They should have made sure their child was provided for beforehand. If the child can't cope on his own he may become involved with a bad crowd and get into trouble. Unless someone is prepared to help him he may be in danger of getting into more trouble and onto the path to addiction, drunkenness or homelessness.

A child may become a nuisance to his family from about the age of nine. Matters will progressively become worse over the years. When he is in his late teens his parents have to tell him to leave and never come back.

That may be an awful action but for the sake of the home they have no choice. The child will be homeless and may become involved with a bad lot or take to drugs or alcohol. Even if he decides to return home he won't be welcome.

Brother Lawrence said that reefer smokers tended to become bad tempered. One smoker (who was white) could be pleasant but had off days. One night he complained to Harry because the record player wasn't working. Harry asked if he had paid which he hadn't and then warned him. Lawrence said he was all right provided he knew where the next reefer was coming from.

Members claimed they could give up reefer smoking at any time but couldn't give up the ordinary cigarettes. If they were asked why they didn't give it up they replied that they had decided not to bother. They may have been unable to admit they couldn't overcome the craving. They were also sending out the wrong message by claiming it wasn't addictive.

Brother Lawrence also told me that reefer smokers were liable to take pep pills. When they could no longer get satisfaction from pills they progressed to the hard drugs such as heroin and cocaine which was really a form of self-destruction. The effect was to increase the rate of the heartbeat. Harry King said that one boy had dropped dead in the club through heart failure. Another boy with a bump on his head didn't have long to live. Sometimes the dealer didn't mix the dose correctly and caused the addict's death. Who can know the thoughts that go through an addict's mind knowing he will die soon and those older than he is will be alive years after he is dead?

Even if they didn't cause death the effect of reefers and pills was that people couldn't control themselves and act rationally. Some siphoned petrol they didn't need. One member stabbed a man while under the influence. Another addict slashed another boy's face with a razor and while in police custody kicked an inspector in the groin claiming he had been assaulted.

One of the things in life that I am most relieved about is that I never started smoking cigarettes. I know how easy it is to get into a bad habit and how difficult it is to get rid of it even if it wasn't that particular habit. If I had started I suspect I would have been a heavy smoker. I don't know if I would have gone onto reefers, pills and hard drugs, terrified of living and terrified of dying. I'm glad I don't know the answer to that question.

What is the solution? It is up to the youngsters to say "No" when offered drugs but that can be easier said than done. A child may feel intimidated to say "Yes" when all the others in the group say "Yes" and assure him or her drugs won't do any harm. If he doesn't he will no longer be part of the group and will have lost his friends. In certain schools a child needs friends for his own protection and if he loses them he is alone and vulnerable. It is easy those who don't face difficult or threatening situations to complain that other people have no spunk in them. However when they are faced with those situations they are also afraid to say "No" and when they are questioned about it they say, "Oh, we couldn't say that."

Once three younger girls came to the youth club. One seemed a better kind of girl who wouldn't become involved with drugs but another was the type who would introduce others to them. Looking back I should have taken the opportunity to warn the first girl who may not have been there before and didn't know about the type who came. I didn't see those girls again and hope she never became an addict.

It is also up to parents to control their children but they don't do so even if they aren't happy about where they go. One girl who attended the youth club said they had told her not to go down there but they were just as bad when they were kids. I said they weren't quite as bad.

One headmaster said that some parents were afraid of their children. If the parents came to see him they said they had gone somewhere else. One father told him to give his son a good thrashing but not to tell he had told him to do it. The headmaster's wife warned about reefers being passed round at parties and said that if the children don't know who is holding the party then they don't go, but how many parents have the courage to take the trouble to stop them? On the other hand can parents supervise them all the time? If they have decided to take drugs they can do secretly by the time their parents find out it is too late.

Parents have been known not even to admit their children do wrong. One parents said that girls are never very naughty despite her daughter's disgraceful conduct in school. When confronted with it they say another child was responsible and they don't face the facts until disaster strikes.

It is possible for schools to exercise influence but how many teenagers listen to those in authority? When I was at school the headmaster in an assembly encouraged the pupils not to smoke but they didn't appear to take him seriously.

What about stringent penalties? A police constable said that the boy who kicked the inspector should have been birched for assault (but didn't mention the attack on the other boy with the razor). I asked Mr King if the birch should be brought back and he said it wouldn't do any harm. Whatever your views on it may be it won't be reintroduced.

In some Asian countries dealers in drugs face the death penalty. People fear death more than prison sentences and it may be better for a few people to be executed than for

many others to die through overdoses or have their lives
ruined. Yet arguments can be made to the contrary. Asian
countries have a lower crime rate in any case which also
applies to drug offences. Statistics can be provided that
show the death penalty doesn't deter but you can prove
anything with them. There again whatever your views on
it may be it won't be reintroduced in Britain.

What can be done to help drunkards, drug addicts and
the homeless? Telling them they are not to drink or take
drugs makes them dig their heels in. They have to make an
effort to rebuild their lives. It is possible to give up
smoking cigarettes by will power and also possible to stop
reefer smoking with greater will power but not everyone
has the strength to do so. Few can get off the hard drugs or
stop drinking meths. Their families don't want to know
them or give them support. The experiences which drove
them to their present state have caused them to be no
longer capable of leading normal lives.

Once they have ended up on the streets some chose to
live there. The outdoor live might be degrading but they
have become used to it and survival is possible. They can
visit the centres for food. At night they sleep in derelict
properties or in the entrances to buildings. One night I
passed a man who warned me that a man was sleeping in
an entrance. He may have felt intimidated but in those
days the homeless didn't pose a threat to others. The worst

that could happen was a request for money. Neither were
the homeless in much danger from others; they were
unlikely to have any money and weren't worth robbing.
The louts might assault them because they loved hurting
people who were defenceless but places where that
happened could be avoided.

During the day they could visit the local libraries and
read newspapers and books provided they were not there
too often. They could sit in the waiting rooms of main line
railway stations and read a discarded newspaper. Best of
all if they had any money they could enter a station on the
circle line of the Tube, buy a ticket for the next station and
travel around all day. They might read a thrown away
newspaper or just sit there. With so many other passengers
they wouldn't be noticed if they didn't sit near the driver or
the guard. At least it was better than being stuck in a job
they couldn't manage or facing rude and abusive people.

If an addict wanted to get off the drugs Harry King
would have helped him. If anyone wanted to work, such as
the man who offered to sweep the crypt, the brothers
would have tried to find him a permanent job.

Occasionally the homeless might have opportunities to
help themselves. At certain times local authorities and
other bodies called for casual workers, such for clearing
the streets after snow falls. A homeless person could take
that opportunity to earn some money if he were able or
willing to do so. Provided he had the sense not to spend it

on drink or drugs he could rent somewhere to live
although the Rent Acts had resulted in available properties
being scarce. Then he could apply for social security
benefits. Through his efforts he would be one rung from
the bottom of the ladder.

Mr King spoke about someone who came to the down
and out centre. His face was so covered in grime that he
thought he was facing a coloured man. However the man
turned out to be a success story and was found a place to
live. He had lovely silvery grey hair and was charming to
speak to. Harry King had taken a bottle of alcohol off him
but when he had been in danger of returning to his old
ways he always picked himself up. That kind of success
story was an exception and in all cases you never know
when a lapse might occur even many years later.

At Christmas a special meal was provided for the
homeless. Mr King said it was a pity that the former down
and out and another who was leading a normal life in
Glasgow could not come and sit at the head of the table as
examples of people who gave up life on the streets.
However the ones who did so never came back to help.

The experience was worthwhile and taught me about
people in spheres of life I would never have known about.
If I had known then what I know now I would have
handled matters differently and might have made more of
a success so far as it was possible to make a success with

that type of kids. Those in the east end of London had the reputation of being the roughest but some people, including professional ones, I've met since have been no better. They may not have been as violent but in other ways were worse. One helper said that if you try to help the east kids they laugh at you. On the other hand I found those kids didn't demand help. Some people require a high standard of helpfulness and politeness from others but repay them with rudeness and abuse. They would be taught a lesson if they had to work in that type of youth club and deal with the east end kids. If they spoke to those kids the way they normally speak to others they would end up with more than broken glasses and might learn to be more polite and considerate to others.

Not long before the youth club closed the church was burned down. Arson was believed to be the cause and, so far as is known, the incendiaries were never found. They may have been disgruntled people who attended the centre or the club or people with no connection. However the church was rebuilt and was reopened about two years later.

Towards the end Harry King said he hoped "I would mention us in your book". He must have assumed my motive in coming to the centre was to obtain material for a book just like the woman at the lunch club. At that time I hadn't considered serious writing. In any event I was only there for a short time and hadn't met sufficient local people and got to know their backgrounds; I didn't have enough information. Someone who written about homelessness had slept with the down and outs to build up his material. Even if I had that opportunity I doubt that I would have been resilient enough.

After I took early retirement I wrote a few stories and found out about the difficulties with publishers. I have no means of finding out if others who went round in search of material succeeded in having anything published. Recently ways of self-publishing on the internet have been established. I have written this article in the hope it may be of interest.

I have left that area and won't return. Now I wonder what happened to the brothers who ran the centre and what they did later; and what became of some of those who attended the homeless centre or the youth club and whether they rebuilt their lives or sunk deeper into depravity. At one time there must have been a home for them where somebody loved them and a welcome awaited them.

Also by this author
Operators of public transport
The Flier (Clapham Junction to Kensington Olympia in the 1960s

9 781548 818333